NEVER FAR FROM WATER

poems by

Rusty McKenzie

First Edition

Cover photo by the author

ISBN: 0-9668455-0-1

Library of Congress: 98-96813

Published by
Sand Bottom Press
W5505 Firelane 12
Menasha, WI 54952

Printed by
Palmer Publications, Inc.
P.O. Box 296
Amherst, WI 54406

ACKNOWLEDGMENTS

I am grateful to the editors of the following publications where some of these poems, perhaps in different form, first appeared:

Wisconsin Academy Review, Fox Cry Review, Rag Mag, Columbia Review, Wisconsin Review, Peninsula Pulse, Wisconsin Poets' Calendar.

for Ellen Kort, Laurel Mills, Helen Fahrbach,
Marge Higgins, and Shirley Anders—
who carried me here

CONTENTS

ONE

TWO

Maybe from the beginning
the issue was how to live
in a world so extravagant

it had a sky,
in bodies so breakable
we had to pray.

—Steven Dunn

ONE

LADIES OF THE AFTERNOON

The day was born
wearing a sullen gray cowl
over its blue face

The terrible voices of crows
called a warning
to the owl in the walnut grove

Now late in the day
there is sun spinning
the amber leaves

and silence lays
pregnant hands on the ladies
of the afternoon

After almond tea and chocolate
they light candles and braid
words into poems, foraging

for phrases ringed with silver
and painted beads, common as bread,
feathered like a wing

They will feed you fire that stings
the tongue, language rising from the dark
to lean against the moon

ON THE EDGE OF DREAMING

She appears to sleep, perhaps to dream
and her mouth, almost but not quite smiling,
tells nothing

because, you see, they have stolen her voice
shut her up, so to speak, in the tower of their babble
their voices curling in and out.

The faces circle her head like a crown. She can't hold
them still—one after another they shift, like chameleons,
from nine years old to fourteen or five, or thirty-three.

One after another, and sometimes in chorus,
prickly voices ring out mom mom mom mom momomomom...
She dreams of quitting her job.

Her head swims through ochre smoke
from the fires she tends without fail. Out on the green
edge of dreaming, the fizz and thunder

of the reckless sea come to light.
She breathes the salt spray, bends to the rhythm of tides,
her throat opens and the song rising in waves

is her own.

ANGEL IN THE HOUSE

It was she who came between me and my paper...
bothered me and wasted my time and so tormented me
that at last I killed her...She died hard.

—Virginia Woolf

I would like to tell you
that I have killed
the Angel in the House
as Virginia Woolf suggests.
But I am not brave.

To say the truth would mean
emptying all my pockets
before wandering into the woods
leaving all the bread crumbs
and shiny white stones
on the back steps

walking into muddy green shadows
without a chocolate bar
or map to find my way back
to the warm kitchen
where lies sleep in tin boxes
lids sealed like dead lips.

Even now I cover my ears
and turn away from the rusty cries
of all those orphaned stories.
A chilly scent of angel wings
settles like smoke
in the folds of my clothes.

THOUGHTS SPUN FROM THE HOMEPLACE

I carry my coffee back
into the bedroom, slip into bed
with Barbara Kingsolver's *Homeplace.*
In these stories boys and young men die.
I think about this, about losing sons,
all the ways it happens.
How Joy refuses to see her son
until he apologizes for treating her badly.
She is brave, angry, sad. Afraid
separation might last forever,
the way it must for Pat and Ellen and Dorothy,
their sons dead too young.
The awful silence, memories bearing down
like sudden storms. I think of my own son,
generous, bright, beautiful, drifting
in mental illness. A careless twist
of chemicals, an imbalance
of something in the brain, they say.
I wonder about sons who go to fight wars.
The mothers...how do they sleep? How
do they pray? Who listens?

IN THIS QUIET SEASON

Stinging
rain
glazes
the driveway
a long
cold weeping
turned
to ice.
Urgent voices
cry
Live fast
in the wake
of all
this dying...
Beyond
the snowline
and the barbed
sorrow
that fences in
these days
I search
for something
holy
for what
grief
might teach.
We wait
as spring
waits
to split
the singing
trees.

SHE TURNS TO PURE MOURNING

-for Ellen

Every day she dips
her hands into mourning
kneading clay   mixing sticks
fur   shells   feathers
scraps of bone
as if to fill the empty room
the spirit dolls come
one after another
raising blind eyes
toward the broken future
their gnarled arms wide
embrace the spirit
of her son stolen young
by some odd plan
as crooked and twisted
as the limbs of weeping
trees that shivered
beside the bay
that terrible Friday
while the moon rode
full-faced and languid
over the cold water
that took him
rocked him for three days
laid him on the shore.

THE LOSS OF A CHILD

As tree shapes from mist
His young death
Loose
In you -Catullus

Shadows spread
across the broad plain
of your face
rivers of clean pain
stream from your eyes
five eagle feathers
crown your long blue hair
a dark star
over purple mountains
smoke rising
from the fire
in your heart
no words strong enough
to break the awful
silence
but the drum
will not be still

A WINTER'S TALE

The woman with snowy hair lives against her will.
Wind rattles the shutters of the house and

winter's rough promise sticks in her throat
like a fish bone that won't go up or down.

She does not speak to her children
about the things that creep across the sill

on a slice of moonlight. She does not name
the dark-eyed bird near the window

or the three-legged dog who sleeps at the door.
She does not tell them what keeps her

awake at night, and in the morning when they sit
in the cold kitchen drinking coffee they say,

the geese are flying early this year—look,
the maple leaves are almost gone.

WEDNESDAY'S RAIN

I watch the rain begin
its long march across the lake

sweeping gray-winged along the far shore
erasing sky, trees, rocks, all the little houses.

No brash thunder, no zigzag lightning
without fanfare it swallows wave after thrashing wave.

Running faster now rain climbs the bank, snapping
the Mayapples' tiny umbrellas, filling tulip cups.

Large drops soak the wooden boards
of the porch floor, washing down the flies

scrubbing away yesterday's dust
like forgiveness, like the absolution of a good death.

WOMANSONG

In the middle of your life
in the midst of all the days
children, cats, jobs, bills, mud—
turn your face
toward the burnished sun

stand away from frayed promises
of bliss and happily-ever-after
listen to forgotten songs
and ancient drums
mockingbirds beyond the walls.

Into the warm river
of your outstretched hands
three angels fall without a sound—
a gift of stillness, gift
of grace, a poem in the afternoon.

WOMANSONG II

She carries home the scent of rain
in her hair, and even after lighting the fire
traces of blue fog hang in the lining
of her thin coat. She sings to the dark
walls, the lace-curtained windows.

Traces of sadness linger in the flowered sheets,
the bowed heads of fiddle ferns. Disappointment,
the sort that comes from failure, imagined
or real. Divorce, years past and still
she says, "I don't think you ever get over it."

She gives herself to children in the city, visits
troubled homes—hard stories at the kitchen table.
In quiet times she watches favorite films,
Cinema Paradiso, Gaslight, Babette's Feast
and kneads the shoreline cedars with her song.

THE WOMAN ON THE GALLERY WALL

Rising up from slick green water
she lowers her eyes, folds her face
into the shadows of her thick yellow robe,
hollow sleeves speak the language
of her journey. Something spills
down the front of her coat like pale milk
leaking from her left breast. A wound
or an offering to a lost child.
She wears the scent of sea and salt
timeless waterstains.

Standing at the edge unable to return
and unwilling to lift her head, blind
to the woman dancing with the raven,
and the path toward the guardians,
the grandmothers, the small boy
carrying a sack of grain, the mother
singing to a newborn baby. She seems destined
to join the other faceless ones, cloaked
and bent, circling the earth's empty bowl.

But if you could touch her
with your sable brushes, raise her face,
find her eyes, she might step from the cold
water to the bold stones along the shore,
ride the bony shoulders of those who
carried her—the ancestors, storytellers,
spinners and weavers, their warm quilts
stitched and ready.

THE DANDELION FIELD

Hundreds of woolly white balls float in the sapgreen
field across the road. As if an invasion of moon children
has taken up residence there, an infestation of luminous
moony heads dropped from a passing space ship.

After supper she leaves plates on the table,
slips on old shoes and walks out. Winnie hears
the door slam, lifts herself from the grass,
comes to claim a headscratch and an invitation
to walk down the lane. Under the aspen canopy,

past the farm where Emma and her new colt browse
behind the barn. Past newly plowed fields, a small marsh
where cattails shelter nesting ducks. Sounds
of red-winged blackbirds and spring peepers. A hawk drops
from the highest limb of a half-naked tree.

She turns back where railroad tracks cross and fade
into evening, south toward Milwaukee, north to Green Bay.
Now and then she bends down to touch wild geranium,
snake grass, the bones of a small animal in the ditch.
Beyond the barn she wanders into the dandelion field.

Tall, bone thin, she walks with a dancer's stride
through seed-laden afterblooms. The hem of her denim skirt
brushes their heads and some of them cling like foam
on the lip of a wave. The moon children nod and bob
as she passes, keeping time with her finespun hum
and the drums of distant hills.

REMAINS UNKNOWN

A one-pound fetus, still wrapped
in its own damp sack, is found by a woman
whose job is to stand all day pulling
oversized chunks from a conveyer belt
that carries the daily waste of Milwaukee's
Metropolitan Sewerage System.

Winter forks its way toward the bus stop
where she stands every day before dawn,
her children and their grandma still asleep.
In the distance the sound of water
washing the feet of the city.

Tonight as darkness folds the streets,
she will stand on another corner waiting
for the bus to carry her home. A loaf
of bread and a bag of apples cradled
in her hands.

CEDAR WAXWING

This is my body, given up for you

Why else would he throw himself
against the windowpane with such determination?
Why else would she find him dead
under a variegated hosta?

This is my body, given up...

she clips the wings with kitchen shears
taking special care of the bright red waxy nibs
on the tips of the secondaries; the wings
luminous as thin gray clouds

This is my body...

twelve slender tail feathers, tipped
yellow as pollen

...for you

the gray and yellow down

She buries the bones under a patch of violets
near the back porch. In an earthen bowl
a nest of feathers, the absent whistle,
the shuddering lightness of wings.

BEFORE THE BLUE HOUR

Whispers begin
as wind slacks off
just before the blue hour
in late afternoon
and always in winter

Always in winter—
yellow leaves asleep
in frozen compost
windows lacy with etchings so fine
they seem sketched
by hummingbird tongues

Then a swelling chorus tongues
the milky rim of memory—
like mockingbirds
melodious, delicate, soulful
One voice, ripens, swims out

Your voice calling
cloudy at first
as if rising through choppy water
then clearing
as clear as water itself
calling my name

ANOTHER DAY

Bittersweet aftertaste of morning dreams...look
death in the face...final exams, my notes fickle and messy...
the teacher is kind, she brings me lunch.

I remember Nancy sitting in the closet counting demons,
long before her grandson died in his crib, long before her hair
fell out, for no reason, they said.

Folded wings of a dove, lemon in the water glass,
four candle flames, a bowl of rice. After the bells of evening
the moon cups Venus in her hand, cradles her there all night.

The apple in your hand drips as you bite, the sound
of seeds spit on the dish like laughter, as if we could survive
beyond the thin strip of mirror that gives us another day.

I will look at you today, even watch you
sleeping, cover my anger and sweep the floor, like an old nun
mucking around in the cold ashes of a useful life.

VULTURES AND BLUEBONNETS

-for Sam Fomon

Three wheeling black vultures throw
shadows into the eyes of two girls lying
as if dead in a field of bluebonnets.

Lower and lower the birds descend
until pale white markings on the wingtips
are clearly visible, the small gray heads

naked and wrinkled, dropping down and down.
Only when thorny feet spring loose to touch
the ground, only then will the girls abandon

their game. Melissa, nine, is the first
to run. Louise, just eight, and already bold,
holds a moment longer.

SEPTEMBER BLUES

Yellow school busses again
on the firelane. Starlings and swallows
gathering. A thumb of dread
invades my bones, as though I might shiver
and die in winter. As if I ever have.

I cradle my pen—my lifeline, my friend,
keeper of secrets and furies, shadows
and surprises. I listen to the clock tick,
rub the tips of my fingers
across the lost days of summer...

But there are no poems today.
No marvelous tales carried from the river
of dreams, even though I saw you there
and kissed your face, still young,
there are no words to call you back.

A STEM OF GREEN

When green is the sound of wind
your hair blows in the east
streams out like seaweed
threading looms of tide

Green comes to live with us
like a cat on raspberry paws
makes herself new
as lovers do in the beginning

STILL LIFE

There's no going back, I suppose,
to innocence, but this seems to be our intention,
what we are drawn to as we leave the road,
make a rough path through the meadow that lies
like an invitation scrawled in twisting grass,
the far trees listening.

Even before wing-shadows sweep the ground
we hear the hawksong keening down
like a warning, a promise, a sign. Caught
in the scream of the circling bird
we stand close together, holding still,
a two-headed woman squinting at the sky.

TWO

MUMBLINGS ON THE NORTH SHORE

There's talk of moving
leaving this house
full of windows
leaving herons, blackbirds
gulls and geese
leaving Winnie
the smell of seasons
firelane walks
and my seven-windowed room
hung in the leafy
canopy of the ravine
where wind and water rattle
and spin the night,
where sun carries
morning over Chandler's hill
and moon comes every month
to sleep on my bed

MORNING SUN

He climbs over Chandler's hill
slides through summer green ravine
down the old elm, dead now
and naked as a grape.
He finds my bedroom window
comes in without a sound

sits on the white wicker settee
that came here from
Granny Bee's front porch,
plays in the leaves
and swings with babies
on the spider plants.

He hides in crystals
that hang near the east window.
Rainbows flash the ceiling
paint photographs across the room
dazzle necklaces on the ceramic rack
I made so long ago.

He traces curls and caves
in sea shells and coral rocks,
alien residents of dresser tops
and window sills. He stumbles
over yesterday's clothes puddled
on the rug, books everywhere.

And when he finds my bed,
falls on blue flowered sheets,

his warm tongue kisses
my sleep-sweet skin
invading dreams
like a jealous lover.

IN THE HEART OF WINTER

A stranger suddenly
at the door, cancer enters
the house. Dropping in
as silently as snow falling
on the wood pile.

Bound to given time
I huddle close to the sleeping earth
listen to winter's heartbeat
try to quiet my mind in whose cage
the dark bird paces.

LEARNING TO PRAY

Late in summer
green and dying
I speak in dreams
as if to see all
I need to learn
when to hold
how to let go

wash of shade and sun
on folding leaves
reminding me
how little I know
of the web I spin
in the house
of wind and sorrow

I DIDN'T WANT TO SEE THE PIPER TODAY

The sound of washing
is the sound of sighing
-Li-Young Lee

When I crossed the Fox
on the Lawe Street bridge
the wail of bagpipes floated
over empty water, and there he was
this young piper, marching
ever so slowly through the fallen
leaves on the river bank.

I wish I were as brave
today as I was yesterday
but now I'm tired again
afraid of the words the doctor said
...treadmill...echocardiogram...
catheterization...surgery...
leaky heart...

Fumbling around
in my confusion...how could I slip
from ripe to rotten
with so little warning?
I stumble into a weedy nest
of feeling sorry, a net of fear
tangled around my ankles.

Last week I told them
about the sign on my wall
that says, I HAVE ENOUGH TIME.
Until I learn once more
what this means

I know I can't say it
so easily again.

                    Defenses crumbling
my voice breaks. I slip
into the blue pool
at the YMCA, the words
of Li-Young Lee's poem
washing through my body, spilling
out my eyes.

                    I listen to my heart
floop floop   floop floop
the sound of fins swimming
in clear blue water, the sound
of the fetal monitor drumming
in the dim loft of a mountain cabin
the sound of life.

JANUARY 1994

days of abbreviated light
days of knife and needles
morphine and surgical stockings
food without salt

APRIL 1994

Here I am, almost well. What to do
with it all—this cobbled heart, these blooming muscles,
prodigal hunger? I look for signs.

Dash of sun, pinch of rain.
A generous wind adopts the cheeky whistle of a blue jay,
ripples the black necklace, tips his cap.

Heron flies low over the lake's quivering skin.
The smell of mud and buds and backyard barbecue, strawberries
from California.

Nixon is dead.
Free elections in South Africa.
Full moon.

Today, even though it's April, winter's old face
refuses to leave the window, a cold mirror, a small wad
of feathers on the glass.

The boys down the road have a new chain saw,
bright red and growling. Five trees fell the first day, pitched
in the ditch with beer cans and condoms. A careless burial.

Because I haven't raked, tulips wear chokers of dry leaves.
Scilla carpets the ground under the blue spruce. A chipmunk lunches
in the live trap.

I scoop it all in
as if the taste of spring will tell me
what really matters.

TALES FROM THE NORTH SHORE

The house stands at the end
of a long dirt lane. A grove
of old walnut trees and broken down fences
hold stories of the land—
how it passed from Indians to Frenchmen
to farmer, papermaker, lawyer ...

Winnebago named the lake, fished
its thick green waters. Voyageurs came
from the Fox and the Wolf. The farmer built
a summer house on the shore, planted
walnut trees, and dug a root cellar.
The papermaker added rooms, wide windows,
gardens for a daughter's wedding on the lawn.
The lawyer fixed the roof, built a deck,
sailed the lake, and let the driveway die,
dandelions and chamomile sprouting
between the cracks. When storms
uprooted trees they lay where they fell
like sad yard art. The fireplace chimney
lost its bricks one by one. Rain came in.
Chipmunks tunneled under the porch,
bees nested in the eaves.

A ripe scent of spring hums through lilacs
and tulips, rub of new green against the sky.
The newly-retired lawyer plays golf, fishes
for trout in crystal cold streams.
On rainy days he watches the Bucks on TV
and thinks about fixing up the house.

CHANGE IN THE WEATHER

pulling myself past the frosty thigh of Autumn
-Anne Sexton

The lake is wild. Chilling
waves roll over themselves, racing
to reach the shore before December
locks the doors. Wind spills
all the yellow leaves, spits walnuts
on the driveway, bonanza for squirrels
building stores. And I'm stalking space,
a tough job for a pack rat. The weight
of these past days has given me sore feet
and a disturbing habit of sighing.
Bees nested under the siding have found
their way into the basement, clinging
all day on window panes, crawling
across the cluttered floor of my dreams.
The cat has turned thin and cranky,
limping more than ever on her gimpy leg.
I fix her favorite treats and pillow
her bed with a heated pad. Still her eyes
are glazed with pain and blame, as if
it's my fault she's always hungry, as if
I could make her young again.

ROOT BOUND

Almost tenderly I scrape away
the skin, dig out blind eyes

toss the potatoes into a pot
of onions, tomatoes, peppers.

There's something good
about handling vegetables

...all those early gardens
Grandpa stringing up beans

Dad pulling the radishes
planted religiously

on Good Friday
come frost or thaw

Mother washing floppy new lettuce
for bacon-laced salad...

I lean on the sink
leaning towards roots

the smell of earth, hot sun,
rain in my hands.

LATE HARVEST

-for Dad

I remember you standing near the rhubarb
one foot crossed over the other
watching birds at the peanut-butter feeder,
a toothpick stuck in the corner
of your mouth, wire-rimmed glasses riding
down the thin bridge of your nose.

Sometimes when the light
is just right and a musky ripe smell
rides the summer wind
I see you there pulling weeds,
moving the sprinkler, arranging the stakes.
Our garden wasn't the best in town
but it fed us well through the summer—
radishes, lettuce, beans, tomatoes, cucumbers,
zinnias and pansies too, if we were lucky.

But more and more these green patches fade
and I listen without hearing your whistle
greeting cardinals and chickadees,
can't remember what you told me
about moon-planting times
or how to choose a juicy melon.
I scratch around in the good rich loam
of childhood like a shadow-gardener
waiting in the rain.

NEVER FAR FROM WATER

I got as far as the eastern
shore. Running away.
Running toward water, slick
and dark. A quarter moon
lay on its side.

The barren beach
a salt-washed place
where endings lie undisturbed
and beginnings wait
for the next wave.

A starfilled night
warm for late September
gentle
like your hands, your life
that slipped away that night

while the quiet moon
tipped upside down
spilling
on the empty beach
the dark water.

A SPRINKLING OF BRIGHT SEQUINS

I wait for the trembling to begin
the way it did yesterday
when I moved the stones

but today is another story
today the sun casts
diamonds on the snow

as if after all there is laughter
behind the glass that gives me back
my face each morning

as if what is necessary
is only as far away
as the tangled roots of memory

Tonight I will plant
a cupful of yellow seeds
under the moon

sleep in the shadow
of the blue fish
love you from a distance

MOTHER DIED ON CHRISTMAS EVE

Roof gone
Walls caving in
Wind enters
    and rain, sun, moonrise
Snow

GHOST STORY

dusty voices rustle the corn
while painted flags of autumn

whip the hard blue sky
sending back summer birds

a randy scent of rotting apple
in the mourning wind

and even though she didn't go
till Christmas it's my mother's

crooked hand that slips through
the sleeve of my sweater

her swollen feet in my shoes
shuffling the leaves

A CHILL IN THE AIR

-for Helen McKenzie, 1898-1990

The cat sweeps her tail across the sky,
children's voices gone from the lake.
There's an itch under my left breast, an ache
in my writing thumb and around my hips.

Granny lies in a hospital bed, speaks
for the first time since her third
congestive heart failure. Released
from machines that breathe for her,
tubes that medicate and urinate,
she asks for her teeth.

"It's awful to get old," she whispers
her voice dry as wind in the corn,
everything goes at once, eyes,
teeth, hands..." Her left eye is closed.
I remember the game we used to play
at family gatherings...

> *the Widow Jones is dead*
> *how did she die?*
> *with one shut eye*

In the emergency room, a respirator
taped and tubed to her mouth

> *the Widow Jones is dead*
> *and how did she die?*
> *with mouth awry*

and how does the rest of it go?

...how did she die?
with leg on high
waving goodby...

Outside, billowing clouds gather
in the autumn sky, a thousand pillows
for her head.

NEW YEAR'S RAIN

I woke on the dark edge
of a day I didn't know
and I knew before my eyes opened

I would not be allowed to enter
again the dream
in which you loved me

Tangled limbs in icy sleeves,
bottomless fog, trees
drifting away one by one

The day grows long without you
and words on the page are mute
never turning to wonder

WELCOME STILLNESS

All of us buttoned and laced
into winter, the house still full
of Christmas, crystal trees and birds
hand carved Santas, ornaments
ribbons and cards...
and I don't want to think about it.
I want a New Year, good and kind.
Last year was hard.

I dream the carefree rhythms
of island life, heartbeat of the sea.
The road through the buttonwoods
buttered with sun and the sweet yeasty
smell of bread from Lola's kitchen.
Hermit crabs snug in their shells,
laughing gulls and mockingbirds,
key lime, tamarind, jasmine.

Low tide
on the beach below the cemetery.
A perfect morning for browsing
through sea scraps. I offer
the first footprints to the sand
and a blessing to the sun
rising on another chance.

THREE

A HALF STEP FROM FLYING

The great blue heron sleeps
like a bag of laundry
on a limb of old elm
high above the damp ravine
still covered with night chill.
Slivers of ice
hem the Winnebago shore.

Far away on the edge
of Dickie's Cay, hot sun
and jelly-green water
wrap around me like wings
and inside
a slumbering bird stirs,
opens one blue eye.

AT SIXTY: PREPARING THE HOUSE

The red wheelbarrow lies in the sand
abandoned after hauling bags
from dock to house that first day.

As if in a single gesture I could shed
old baggage, but like a conch crawling the seabed
I wear a mossy shell, leave a crooked track.

  a bowl of lemons on the table
    a shimmering glaze of sun on the sea
      tonight a half-eaten moon

No newspaper, TV, radio, phone. Alone
I swim with angelfish, sting ray, turtle, shark,
write poems for lovers found and lost.

My hair grows wild as a moonring. I scrape
the faded paint from this old Bahamian cottage
rooted in the rock of Dickie's Cay.

Change is no stranger here. The house
gives up its yellow coat and years fall away
like memories washed in sand.

CASTAWAY

Moonless night, wind asleep
Stillness settles
like a feather
in my open hand

On this small island
anchored in the Sea of Abaco
I begin again to love
the geography of solitude

SNORKELING AT DICKIE'S CAY

dipped in gin-clear sea
  ageless and weightless
    my skin dissolves

spreads like water
  silky-green translucent
    fluid

awash in seahash
  wrinkled rainbows
    dimpling the sand

sunshafts starfish conch
  turtle grass sponges
    myriad luminous fish

drifting in sea-space
  I hear
    clicks and squiggles

crunch and snap
  of trunkfish
    nibbling coral nubbins

tapping out a story
  a poem perhaps about
    the lunacy of human divers

who try to loosen
  the mystery of fish—
    counting and naming

IF YOU CAN'T STOP THE HURRICANE

the tail of the storm whips
the island steel wind thundering surf
scent of rain and salt
no docile captive I strip
the last barrier between the wind and me
slip into the sea without shame or malice
water touches me everywhere

my arms fan out
like fins slicing waves
sucking a lungfull of air
I tuck my chin lift my hips
in a rush of foam
I pull the water over my head
dive into sudden stillness

drifting slowly toward the next breath
I face the storm
from the belly of the sheltered cove
rain dimples the waterskin
like the tears of lost children
nailing down the sea
all that brief light shining through

SAND ART, LOVE IN THE ISLANDS AND THE CERTAINTY OF TIDES

Sea wind
rubs
the tip of a thin
blade of grass
across the face
of the barrier dune
carving
a perfect crescent
beside the broad stroke
of longleaf blolly
the everlasting sand
surrenders
pennywort doodles
and sea oats
kneel
drawing wings of heron
under a purple sky
all this vagrant
stroking
and yielding
turns me to water
I marry the sea

RIDING THE DOLPHIN

Night birds hum and snore
while ghost crabs drum the beach
opening the sea.
Windows foggy with the breath
of cats singing to November stars.
Steam pours from the pasta pot
the tea kettle and the sheets
in which we roll until it seems
we swim under water, and time
hangs on the back of a chair
like a piece of string.

PAST PELICAN CAY

Waterstars ripe as summer,
slick and fat as butter spread
on tumbling waves. Voices fall
overboard, plumb the night sea.

If only I could reel back the words
spoon them up like pudding, taste
the caramel moon that drags the sea
like a bag of salt.

So many dreams...How much we wished...
Endings, it seems, are never enough,
never long or sweet enough
when the story is so damn good.

SONG THAT LIVES IN A CHAMBERED SHELL

However hard you may search for it
you will never be able to grasp it
you can only become it. -Ikkyu

Maslow called it ecstasy. Saints call it God. Mystic, witch, shaman, snake handler, madwoman, healer—all tell the story. Mine goes like this:

Bahamas. A moonless night in the late sixties--
our boat sails easily through the dark water.
An occasional light winks from passing islands.
Long after the others have gone below I sit
at the rail watching the wake slide by, churning
dark into light. At first I name it: phosphorescent
plankton. Then I embellish, call it stars-in-the-sea.
Words wash away in rustling water, every splash new
against the faceless sky. I grow large and empty.
The night's poetry fills the split between me
and out-there...and for a time that has no name
I see with eyes of water, wind, stars—know
the lesson of wings.

SHARK

I hang on the ceiling of the sea
twenty feet above the sandy floor.
Masked eyes wary.

A dark shape plows the reef
glides out over white sand, shoving
water aside with its head.
Long muscled body, wide-spaced eyes
tail of shark.

I remember asking Skeet, What should
I do if I see a shark? Look at it,
he said, and admire the wonder
of this beautiful animal. Then go
about your business. No fuss.

I tell myself it's a nurse shark
try to imagine it wearing a white cap,
holding a blood-pressure cuff.
Emerson says nurse sharks are vegetarians.
I try to believe.

Shark and I measure the space between us.
I force myself to breathe. Shark rises
...looks at me...I look at shark...and
for one fearless moment we are only curious.

A TIME OF BELONGING

Taking an unexpected turn
we ride north
through the harbor
on the tail
of a bottlenose dolphin.
Past Edwin's Boat Yard
and Albury's Sail Shop
past the tangled mangroves.
Just before Dilly Cay
she turns into the creek
and of course we follow
this pearly smooth creature
who showers us with blessings
each time she leaps.
                Listen
                     to the sweet *whoosh*
         of her breathing
There is something here
that takes us back—
something familiar in this
watery song as powerful
as love and hunger.

THE WOODCARVER

If you were to ask, he might tell you stories
of his journey from trials and wills
to bananaquits and pelicans

Trade winds carry the scent of salt
and cinnamon to the woodcarver rocking
on the porch of the yellow house, wood chips
spread around him like a nest of moth wings.
He props his bare feet on the railing
near a bowl of sweet raspberry tea,
his daily offering to bananaquits who fly in
to watch the flick of his knife.

Morning sun flings red coins on the water.
Palms and buttonwoods wink and shine
like old crystal. The woodcarver whistles
and jiggles his feet, twists the blade
mapping his way to the pelican hiding in pine.
Pale shavings rain down his belly, cover
his clothes like feathers and when he walks
they speckle the rooms of his house.

Even though this pelican will not ride
the high thermals or sing lullabies
at the breeding grounds, never lock its
webbed toes onto a piling, steal from
lesser anglers, plunge into a school
of mullet, or see wind spin a waterspout,
this pelican will fly

from the wood, set free by the woodcarver
feathering the wings, unlocking the hungry beak.
He stops whittling only when bananaquits come
to sit on the rim of the tea bowl.

He calls them by name, *Curly...Whitey...*
coaxes them to his hand, his low voice
crooning *trust me, trust me...*

THE TATTOOED DIVER

The brass bell
at the end of the dock
announces his coming.
Hood pushed back
his yellow slicker hangs
open to the soft kiss
of rain falling on the island.

She stands on the porch
wearing a sassy red shirt
and a slow smile
a little embarrassed
but far too curious now
to care.

What does he carry
in his outstretched hands?
Funny, she doesn't see
the shiny wet snappers,
the inevitable feast
that will fill their plates
for many nights.

SPOTTED EAGLE RAY

I swim over the coral head
where rainbow parrotfish graze
the crystalline sea as green as it gets

bulbous eyes of balloonfish follow me
past the grouper hole, past the point
where windy currents skirt the cove

I swing out over a stretch of sand
shaved and carved
as if by desert winds

all at once a monstrous eagle ray—
white spots like pearls across its wide black back
a starry kite from the night sky

here we are, each of us wandering
the shallow sea alone, nothing between us
but a handful of water

we do not shy away
from this fragile meeting
sweet watermusic singing in our ears

I wave my blue fins, he fans
dappled wings, glides under me
and when our eyes meet

I think he might rise up
carry me away...and then he's gone
like yesterday's easy innocence

IN THE LAND OF RED HIBISCUS

Dickie's Cay, 1997

Hibiscus dances the tango that breaks
each day without fail, the one that lights
the morning lamp, releases us from darkness,
drums us into daytime.

A carnival of dreams still warm
on my pillow—I try to keep them
in bed with me, but they fall into shadow
like the moon between wax and wane.

I wake too late to watch hibiscus fan
her flaming skirts, unwrap the spear
bedded in the dark, its lacy yellow collar,
its crown of blazing stars.

Coconut palms loop and sway, a tattoo
of island stories dressing the sky
in juicy blue-green language, sweet as honey
on my winter tongue. Sunlight chooses a petal here,

a leaf there, a certain patch of sand
until the green sea swallows the last light and
hibiscus twists her dress for the last time
blessing her one and only perfect day.

When I turn off the light
there is only darkness and the smell of sea,
leaves rattling their beads,
stars sipping coffee, eating

the night's sweet licorice,

and out beyond the open shutters
the sky shamelessly flaunting her finest
charms and spangles.

YOU TAKE YOUR CHANCES

Frigate birds fly low.
Soon bitter wind will sweep
a wicked broom across the island.
We watch the ragged sky
and talk about danger

the sort that Judy and Roy will face
next year when they set out alone
in their shiny new catamaran
for the long Atlantic passage
Portugal to Abaco.

We recall the night with no stars
when the sea turned rough and the wind
blew us into deep troughs and over
the top of climbing waves. We abandoned
the race when the OSPREY called
May Day...May Day..Mayday.mayd...

Here in the vital bath of island sun
we read *Into Thin Air* and taste madness.
All those chilling stories, threads
in the tapestry of death-by-adventure.

Considering the odds, other ways
to go—hospitals, nursing homes, boredom—
we plan our next gamble, even though
we know that maps and schemes are made
of fragile stuff, subject to sudden change
by what we cannot name.